CASINO OF THE SUN

CASINO OF THE SUN

Jerry Williams

Carnegie Mellon University Press
Pittsburgh 2003

Acknowledgments

The following journals and anthologies were kind enough to publish selections from this book: *Lyric, Crazyhorse, Mudfish, American Poetry Review, Negative Capability, Press, Exquisite Corpse, Orpheus, Now This, Mississippi Mud, Seems, Barrow Street, Sundog: The Southeast Review, Sycamore Review, Poems & Plays*, and *Signs of Life: Channel Surfing Through 90s Culture*.

The author is grateful for permission to include the following previously copyrighted material: an excerpt from "Down in the Bottom" by Willie Dixon. Copyright © 1995 by Hoochie Coochie Music (BMI)/administered by Bug Music. All rights reserved. For additional information on the genre of the blues, please contact: The Blues Heaven Foundation (founded by Willie Dixon in 1981) 2120 S. Michigan Avenue Chicago, Illinois 60616 Phone: (312)808-1286/Web: www.bluesheaven.com

To Jonathan Ames, Adam Braver, Gerald Costanzo, Kevin Gonzalez, Susan Hee, John Kintz, Cynthia Lamb, Lisa Lewis, Tyler Lewis, the New Jersey State Council on the Arts, Steve Orlen, Bill Ratner, Richard Shelton, Rosalie Siegel, Patricia Taylor, and Tim Vukelic— many, many thanks.

Book design by Tyler Lewis

The publication of this book is supported by a grant from the Pennsylvania Council on the Arts.

Contents

for my mother

Meet me in the bottom.
Bring me my runnin' shoes.

–Willie Dixon,
from "Down in the Bottom"

I. A Fine Powder

A Fine Powder

He had a little box that looked like a dark brown treasure chest
with an iron gargoyle for a lock.

He had a grainy whetstone that he kept
in an aqua blue pouch with Chinese lettering.

I have no idea who he was; he died and I'm getting paid
to tear the dry wall out of his house with a claw hammer.

That box has a red velvet lining; it's got keys in it, matches,
the tassel from a graduation cap.

There's no money, not that I would take it,
but there's a spent shotgun shell
and a pink guitar pick with teeth marks all over it.

I can't promise that I won't demolish this house.
Delicateness makes me lonely and loneliness makes me vicious.
I keep a sledgehammer in the truck.

But undoubtedly a pattern exists here.
A dead man lies in state, his face clean-shaven, expressionless.

The telephone rings and a familiar voice says,
Do you still have my knife?

Undoubtedly, a pattern.
Maybe it's better to disavow the small things.
The opposite of a miracle hovers above this spare estate,
looking for a tongue, a teller.

Casino of the Sun *for the Markovich brothers*

It's Christmas day in Arizona:

one hundred and sixty degrees above zero and rising.

When you get off the plane,

which you secretly hoped would crash,

and pass through that gray chute,

your old roommate, the Chin, greets you,

lathered in the ocher of a different time zone.

Nakedly joyful, a boy of ten or eleven

jumps into his father's arms.

A camera flashes and the Chin snorts,

Another chat room dream come true.

Close your eyes, imagine giving birth

to a thousand mallard ducks inside a shark cage

while some non-union uniform runs a metal detector

up and down your leg, up and down your other leg.

Welcome to hell. Try not to spill your margarita.

Try not to let the molten parking lot solidify

in your lungs when you hear about your ex-girlfriends

riding the cranks of hard-minded day traders

in Mustique or Minorca

or wherever people go who have parents.

There's a bed waiting for you in the desert,

though the sheets were not prepared for your arrival.

The cordless phone is dead,

but the cable television works fine.

Shaquille O'Neal just missed another free throw,

and we all know why. He brings the ball

too close to his face; he smells his fingers.

He's distracted by his own good fortune.

Those guys have it made: ballplayers.

The Chin says they live like dolphins.

Shaq, Sprewell, Allen Iverson. Sweet.

What am I doing here anyway? This is not my affair.

I've drunk blood from a leopard print purse,

said *I love you* under my breath,

shared an apartment with a terrified and weeping,

uprooted fleshpot

who caught me looking at pictures of lepers.

I have checked the pulses of dead husbands

and disagreed with the diagnosis,

listened through walls for signs of forgiveness,

been counted on and let down and squeezed out.

I bet I would sell my organs in China,

I would build electric chairs for a dollar an hour

if I could only put together enough scratch

to go back in time and burn the right bridges.

By next Christmas, I vow to pledge my life and mind,

my entire troubled essence,

to a beautiful cyborg with reliable taxonomy

and skin the color of grape soda.

But for now, the Chin toasts the end of an era

in a bar on the edge of effectiveness.

A lonely jingle leaks out of the sound system,

and the patrons sing along like there's no tomorrow.

Every Sunday morning they wake up

with inexplicable cuts and scrapes on their hands.

These are your people.

They would offer you the world

if they had any right to it.

Gaps, Guns, Targets

There are gaps in my memory,
and guns. A rack of three
on the wall in my parents' bedroom,
and one next to the Vaseline
and the heating pad in their nightstand.

The rifles I never touched,
but sometimes I would take
the revolver out of the drawer
and hold it in my hand.
It was surprisingly heavy
and the grip was covered
with sharp little bumps.
I never aimed at anything
(there were bullets in an ashtray).
I just held it and gazed at it,
my heart pounding in my head.

If my father had discovered me,
he would have shot me
to teach me not to play with guns,
like when he killed my bicycle
with a sledgehammer after I crashed

going down the hill by our house.
That's how he was.
His answer to everything
was a dollar bill;
or the sight of him
charging you like a bull
with drool backed up in its eyes,
yanking his belt through
the loops of his pants with a flourish
and the snap of leather;
or else it was wrapped
in a red oilcloth next to
the Vaseline and the heating pad.

There must have been times
when he imagined
wiping us all out—
my mother, my sisters, and me.
Times when he'd get one
of those dizzy spells
and hate would not suffice,
and we started looking
more and more like targets.

A Pleading

Why can't I be cleansed?
By cleansed I mean something more important
happening to me.
John the Baptist could cleanse me
but they cut his head off just for fun.
And going to Jesus is exhausting.
Must I be touched
by the hands of an innocent,
whose life is indescribable,
before I can no longer feel
the hole in my vessel?

I don't see the difference
between restitution and renewal.
Bright orange gulags
inherit the swag.

Can love cleanse?
The right kind.
Can other people be your salvation?
Maybe.

I see these old couples on TV

(my only contact with the aged).
The woman is in a hospital bed,
eyes closed, the picture of serenity,
hooked up to the dying machine.
The doctor pronounces the words:
"There's nothing we can do."
The man begins to cry.
It's been forty years since he last cried.
He confesses he's not ready
for her to go yet.
The cockatoo will keep saying her name.
The doctor's eyes move.
"There *is* one other option.
A new procedure, very experimental.
We could attach you both
to the dying machine."
The old man keeps saying her name
but he isn't looking at her
or listening to the doctor.
What was her name?
Something that sounds like *rise* or *lies*.
They'd been taking long walks
when the sun was about to come up.
They hardly slept.

Trash

I am dealing with my grandmother's
dead mattress in the garage
and I can't remember her maiden name.
A week ago, under this bare bulb,
she swept cigarette butts, insect carcasses, and soot
into a rounded pile, rehearsing.
I don't think it could be said
that she was ever a beauty,
but at the end the woman looked exactly
like hell. She pickled herself
on TV juice and little purple guys:
some doctor's idea of the twilight years.
Waking up delirious in the hospital,
she gulped down a handful of imaginary pills.
No reason to go on after that.
She willed her own death,
as though she'd propped the broom against the wall
and stepped back inside the house.

Today the sky is so white it's invisible.
I grip the mattress by the edges,
drag it out to the curb.
My grandmother was always sick or nervous

from what I remember.
Aunt Jean got her stoned once;
I don't think she liked it.
She had a relationship with god
that nobody cared to fathom.
She was 62 when she died. I stared
at the hymnal and followed the words
to the same songs as the last funeral,
her son's.
I never knew her and I have lost her,
and I am trash.
I let the mattress drop to the ground
with a thud and a billow of dust.
Real and imagined,
there was a lot of pain in this bed.

Good Vibrations

There was the propeller
and there was the bowl of acid.
They both had black hair
and I tried to ravish them,
they looked so graceful and inviting.

There was the Amazon breast nailed to the front door,
blood dripping onto the welcome mat.
She must have hit star-69.

If I was ever going to rise up, something yellow had to happen.
Is it possible to ridicule beauty?

A dead crow lay in the parking lot,
flat as a no from god,
one suspicious wing aflutter in the breeze.

An old friend stopped by for coffee.
Coming up for air, he said,
and there were tears in his eyes from the smell.

This was by no means a normal Saturday afternoon.

My lungs weren't dipped in boiling copper.
I didn't sit on the couch in my underwear
cleaning the shotgun and watching cartoons.
I sipped my harmless coffee, made goo-goo eyes at eternity,
waited for night to pull up to the gate
and honk its horn.

Harlan County Copula

My mother walked me by the wrist,
limping, back to the farmhouse,
her thickly freckled hand cold
as though she'd leaned against a headstone
in the cemetery where the dead
of this hollow lie buried.

We were either on the moon or in Kentucky,
visiting second cousins.
The drive south seemed all downhill
until we reached Pine Mountain.
That was the summer the coal miners
at Brookside and Highsplint struck.
The UMWA marched through the streets
of Harlan with pickaxes reflected in their eyes.

I'd spent the day with Robby at the creek,
catching crawdads in butter bowls
and blasting them with rocks at close range.
The water being warm, we went shoeless,
and I sliced the milky arch of my foot
on a broken Pepsi bottle.
Until I came out of the water

and saw my footprint
on the bank filled with blood,
there was no pain.

Across town a miner lay on a blanket of blood
and stared into the sun with his eyes stuck,
no longer complaining,
no longer on the clock,
quite unaware of the movie camera
that snored in the sickbed of history,
unaware of my mother putting her hands
around my waist and lifting me up
to the kitchen table
which I must have mistaken for sky.

Breeding and Feeding

I would just as soon not eat. It's a pain in the ass. I wish I could take a jar of paste three times a day like a good astronaut and get all the nutrition I need. Maybe that's where we'll end up, but for now I eat the regular stuff. Peanut butter, broccoli, milk, tongue, crackers, black beans. I feel like I'm feeding. It's disgusting, I eat so fast. My ex-girlfriend used to say– we'd be sitting at the table– "Did you even taste it?" She'd give me the you've-got-to-change-this-behavior look. Right through my eyes to the back of my skull. I had to get out of that relationship. Sometimes I dine with people, they look up, I've cleaned my plate, I'm sipping my water (I love water). They say, "What the hell?" I know, I eat fast, it's disgusting. They've barely had time to spread their butter and bug the waitress for more syrup. I can't help it. I want to get it over with and go on with my life. Am I afraid the food will abandon me? When I was a kid my father would take the whole family out to Ponderosa Steak House. I was named after the owner, who was a man my father admired. We'd go through the line, order number four or number six, sit down to eat. He'd always start in on everyone else's dinner when he finished his own. That hairy forearm coming across the table like a missile. We had to sit there and take it. My mother said, "Dave, why don't you leave them kids' food alone?" "We'll get 'em another one," he grunted. Which never happened. The trick was to shove the steak and french fries down your neck before he could get his mitts on them. That's why I eat faster than a slot machine. But I'm clean. Don't let anyone tell you different. If you sat me down to lunch with my namesake and the ex-girlfriend, I wouldn't spill a thing. She could tell him how long I've been waiting to meet him. How proud I am to be named after a steak house baron.

He'll pick up the check. Pay off all my student loans. On the way home the ex-girlfriend whispers in my ear. Soft. Inhuman. She'll try to end the famine in my blood. Somebody bless her. Before she opens her eyes.

Elegy for Samuel Beckett

Artichokes make me feel predatory.

Tendons erupt, retinas scramble–

I twist myself into a Bengal tiger

swiping at a dead horse carcass

with my claws of yellow bone.

The meat gets softer near the heart.

Blood turns Jamaican rum vermilion.

Shit! Across the vain savanna

a raunchy telephone rings once, twice.

I growl high in my throat, rise from the table,

and answer it. The voice at the other end

unleashes the terrible news:

He died a week ago in Paris.

I try to grieve, to simply tip over onto the floor,

but the closest I ever came to him

was three one-acts at the Harold Clurman Theatre

in New York, 1985, and the pages of his book.

I keep a picture of Beckett above the oven

where the ceramic rooster used to be.

In the picture, he's sitting on a footstool

in the corner of an empty room

with a cigarette between his fingers.

He's wearing worn-out hush puppies
and a frayed v-neck sweater.
He looks predatory.
And here I am, some stiff, gazing into the eyes
of a man who lived in a renovated prison,
a man who insisted on wearing Joyce's shoe size
even though it was two sizes too small.
Practically everyone I know wanted to *be* him
whose final sigh must have been deafening.
Samuel Beckett knew what no one else knew—
and now he knows this.

Style   *for Louise Parms*

Winter approaches like a retaliation
and I wonder will it be as bad
as the last one. Lodged in a stupid room
with a borrowed bed and dresser,
ensanguined clock radio numbers,
imaginary rope and wobbly chair.
Repeating the alphabet to pull my heart rate
down and the sun back up in the sky
so I can at least go to my job
and pretend I'm not splattered.

My sister said, *I don't even feel like
I have a brother. Where's he been?*
And it's cold and gray where I am,
and there's a buzzing sound.
I'm learning how to stop trying
to get my old life back
when I haven't yet found a new one.

It's funny to think
of what keeps us going.
Is it the hope of something better
or just the hope that someday
we'll be able to handle what there is?

Portland Is No Place for the Soulless

Across from the YMCA I have found
somewhere to park until morning.
Behind glass, healthy human bodies run in circles
and hoist weighted bars above their heads.
It all looks magnificent.
As individuals, I presume, they are decent people
with homes and jobs, maybe husbands and wives.
I do not resent them.
I think of you, Rosamond,
and 839 Formosa Avenue.

I got drunk on wine tonight
at the Salmon Street Bar & Grill
with the day bartender. You get drunker
than usual in those kind of places.
You're watching a game on television,
your blood starts pumping a little harder,
and all you can do is drink.

Compelled somehow like a piece of meat
being forked into an open mouth,
I came up here to get away,
as they say, find an apartment and a job.

I considered Boise, but I'd heard Portland
has a river running through the center of town.
Now I'm drunk and alone
in a strange green world—
so far from Los Angeles, so far from Ohio.

If I crawl in the back seat and fall asleep
I might never wake up,
so I open the door and work my way out of the car.
It's darker than the inside of a fist.
Shuffling into the woods, I unzip my trousers
and pull it out, urinate, and then jack off, crying,
my shoulder against a tree. Anything to forget
who I am for five minutes.

Large Father Syndrome

A battalion of blondes and their hairless
captain of desperation take the wrong trail

in a sold-out nightmare,
gasping for light,

sharpening gray bayonets and eating
breakfast out of half pint-sized cans.

In the sand near the water,
amid the melange of lorry tracks,

cracked spectacles, roots and thorns,
a tender worm migrates

through this movie of absolution.
Focus on the detour past a pair

of shabby, tightly-laced jungle boots.
No wings anywhere.

Something must be waiting
under the rocks at the gate,

scratching words in the universe:

never never never never

arrive.

II. Matisse Room

Matisse Room

Color

In a smack red room
with garish curtains
mantling the window,
a Matisse painting slides
off its canvas into place.

Conjuring Jealousy

When we aren't there it doesn't exist.
No one can sleep on the bedding;
no one can scatter clothes on the floor.
I believe we are jealous of the room.

Nomads

You said, Which room is it?
This one, I said, and I followed you in.
At that moment I knew I loved you.
I did not know a thing about love
until we walked into the room.

Harvest

If we stay in the room and plant
tomatoes and watermelon near the closet
and lilies near the window,
we must wait patiently for the harvest.

Divertimento

I have poured too much in your glass;
nevertheless, you will probably drink it.
When we make love in Matisse room
some of it spills over the side.
We empty it and fill it up.

The Revolution Was Romantic

The Russian room to the north changed its name.
Then ranking members entered to discuss
whether the urinals would be communal or enclosed.
Trotsky lobbied for enclosure.
Lenin wanted them to be made of gold.

Chance

Some mechanic took apart an airplane
and left the pieces in the room.
When we saw them we thought
we were in the wrong fur shop.

Not Enough Room

Joseph tried to get Mary in.
A camel tried to get in.
Derain and Marquette tried to get in.
A ship full of Jews tried.
But only you and I could get in.

Morning, Noon, and Night

Children leap out of corners
and wrestle each other to the ground.
Children alone in the room
are never frightened,
are never alone very long.

The Collarbone Defense

You had been living in a room
down the hall to the right
in which the floor and furniture
were covered with adhesive plaster.
I was born in the room directly
below it several years later.
Fearing the stone-blind financial
beast screaming and chomping
on its own flesh, you could
never take me near your room.

Another Chance

Anyone who had ever been in love
wandered into the room by mistake
and ended up talking about Cocteau,
Matisse, salad dressing, and other lovers.

Denial

I cannot be sure but I think Philip Glass

was on the stereo when your glass
was upset, spilling its contents.
After we left the room the music stopped;
certainly, you recall, Matisse room
does not exist then.

Oracle

When I inquired about the sudden disharmony
she replied, I am not an oracle.

Dead Reckoning

Windows are open for the night.
The hallway is quiet
but for the red-handed voices.
We are in a room together,
a room far away from the others.

Coming and Going

No one could leave the room.
Vlaminck couldn't get out.
A ship full of Jews couldn't get out.

The trapper couldn't get out.
Only you and I could get out.

Dream

The room had a dream. Or I had a dream.
An accurate woman combed her hair
in front of a mirror that was exactly
the same size as her body. Balconies
collapsed and fell around her.
The French professor hid behind
a torn-out car seat and threw mudballs
at moving targets. The room felt
like a department store during a clearance sale.

Tire

Cut in two.
Twisted and entwined on the floor.
We look like a tire in the room.

Roomer

A drifter with something bad

in his past moved into the next room.
We often hear him talking unabashedly
on the telephone at inappropriate hours.
We suppose, by the inflection in his voice,
that he's talking to people who know us.

The Voices

I don't know if I am allowed to love you.
I wish things were different.
Turn on the light. Brighter.
Yes, as a matter of fact, that is
precisely what I was thinking.
How did you know? Forget it, I know.
There are no clouds in the sky of the room.

Melancholia

It's round and large
and it's on wheels
and it's wooden and dark inside.

Reformation

So, I'm not quite 21
and I'm overcome by you.
The beer and vodka
should help us decide
what to do with our lives.
Let's save ourselves
future dismal Thursdays;
let's stop all this desperate
running from room to room
and go back to where we have
previously shown each other
much kindness.

III. Self-Portrait in a Knife Blade

Afternoon at the Ex's

She cleaned her apartment
and did laundry
while he played records.
Some old stuff–
Schumann, Roy Orbison.
They'd been apart
three months.
A rope burn of regret
seared his duodenum.
Some call it starting over;
some call it losing everything.
He was recovering from the flu,
she came near him
to pick up a dirty bath towel,
and he kissed her.
You probably shouldn't do that,
she said, And besides, you're sick.

Afternoon turned thoughtlessly
into evening.
The two of them lay
on her bed,

which was more comfortable
than his own,
and made beautiful deceit
to the steady canticle of apologies.
It was the saddest
erection he ever had,
inside the latex prison
of infrequent lovers.

They slept afterwards,
and he had a dream.
They were walking across
a bridge above a river
and came upon a truck wreck.
Gasoline was everywhere,
but the driver had it
under control with a squeegee.
There was music coming
from the cab of the truck
and she started dancing
along the edge of the bridge,
motioning for him.

As he approached,
her right foot slipped
and she fell off.
He watched her unbrazen descent.
At first she was terrified,
then something else
came into her eyes.
He didn't know whether to jump
over the side or make his way
down to the riverbank.
He woke up before he could
do anything.

In the hard darkness
he listened to the familiar
curve of her breathing.
He didn't want to,
but he kept running
that look on her face
through his mind.
The look that said
I know you didn't mean

to hurt me.
The look that said
I understand
but I'm going, I'm going.

Touch

I wish I hadn't called.
The second you heard my voice
you went off like a car alarm
through the agonized beeps and bells
of your anchorite melody
that everyone hates but lives with.
I should have known you'd keep me
on the phone trying
to avenge four years of no contact.
You haven't changed.
Listening to you tell me you're a better writer,
louder talker, more dispirited and friendless,
isn't my idea of forgiveness.
You win.
I admit I envy the rock fight going on in you,
the categories and sub-categories
of irritation and rage,
your heart wet-slapping against your skull.
I dream I'm you sometimes,
sitting at an old typewriter
composing the airline jingle that'll make me
so rich I'll buy you a new spleen.
Will you go away now?

Honestly, I'm afraid of you.
I'm afraid you'll move in with me
and pick up where we left off.
I can hear blowing out and tamping in.
The phone line starts to burn
and I lose my place.
I loved you so much,
but something happened.

Giving In

The expression on my face
doesn't know who I am.
My need, a brooding locomotive,
vibrates in the heat.
All the ceiling fans in this bitter
lounge run on dread.

The waiter brings another miracle.

Back in my apartment
the telephone is cranking up
the end of the world.
Electricity stupefies the spider plant.

I might be expected to shave my head
now that the only radio station in town
plays nothing but train songs
with terrible precision.
My other life turns on a spit
in the courtyard of loneliness.

The Book of Threats says not to hesitate.

I should wipe the flames out of my eyes
and go home.

Self-Portrait in a Knife Blade

I wish I had no mother, no father, no sisters,
no uncles and aunts, no cousins, no grandparents,
living or dead.
I wish I had no friends in L.A., none in San Francisco,
no friends back in Ohio,
no friends' friends, nobody.
I wish I had no woman.
I wish I had no bosses, no liquor store clerks,
no landlady in a housedress and hospital slippers
trudging up to my door.
I wish no one lived down the hall from me.
I wish I didn't owe anyone anything but money.
I wish I had no telephone,
no U.S. Mail.
I wish my impossible car would die
in the middle of an intersection
before a hundred honking horns and twisted faces
and I'd just walk away from it.
I wish the devil or god
would come up here or down here
right now
and try to fuck with me.
There's no transition.

When my eyelids commence
their involuntary semaphoria,
I hope the plastic horizon shudders.
If I had a black magic marker,
this would all be over in about ten seconds.

Boneyard in Absentia

I can't talk or write or fuck or fight
or love or shoot my way out of this one.

I hide like a bug in the wall;
I stink like a prehistoric dog.

Chased away from the pack of liars,
not speaking unless spoken to,

because I ride my skull around and never sleep
and my eye's hanging down.

I want the scene to leave to leave the scene

Is a man's shadow being made
or is the shadow making the man?

Would you blame the bees if they stung
us all till we died and would you blame

the rats and birds if they naturally
came along and picked the dirty bones clean

and would you blame the hounds
if they buried the proof in mounds?

Emerald Lake

At ten thousand feet
the water was clear enough for us to see
where the trout's wings used to be.
The air was uninfected, so we took off our masks.
My ridges smoothed over
as the street headache waned.
When I opened my eyes all the way
the trout was swimming down a small waterfall.
I knew it was a felony to think of eating meat
but I couldn't help it, I couldn't help it.
I'd sweated and groaned inside my godless manhole;
I'd saved my Valium Dollars for eight years to see this.
Soon the sun would be a brown dwarf,
this lake would start to coagulate,
and the trout would need to be vacuumed up
and discharged in a jewelry store at street level
with the rest of the precious gems.
Ludicrous would have his way with the world.
To my guide I said, "Trout used to be silver, right?
What color are they now?"
"I don't know," he said.

Dispatches from the Shelter

Everything began to tremble—
like the face of an insect.

★

Whenever you want something
you will never possess it,
even if you stop wanting it.
The object of your desire
eats you, drinks you, expels you.

★

Knowing I have this reckless need for her lips,
the scar, the scent of her hair.
Knowing she has an answering service
and sometimes I call just to hear
the patience in her voice.
Am I trying to befriend the warden?

★

I want to be buried in a Cadillac.

★

Since she was bleeding, we did it anyway.
When we finished I ran my finger
through the blood that coated my penis
and applied it to my face like war paint.
I did my best Indian squall,

dancing around her on the bed.
That I was serious goes without saying.
She thought I was crazy,
but she laughed and laughed.

★

Don't you want to move to New Zealand,
the island, with me?

★

A carnivore masquerading as a herbivore,
a social climber in hermit rags.

★

We were playing a game
in which we tried to embarrass
and humiliate each other
by bringing up things from the past.
She wanted to convince me
that this is the one exception
to an otherwise virtuous life.
She's one hot pilgrim.

★

If our language were foreign,
we couldn't hurt each other.
I'll make edgy love to you

and breathe with you.

I no longer need to speak to you.

★

A strand of hair floats to the ground.

In agony.

★

Maybe you could have loved me.

★

I don't want your voice in my head any more than I wanted

Mrs. Webster's voice in my head in the third grade.

This is a veiled attack on my beliefs.

Such as they are.

★

She called me from a payphone.

(Pouring down rain,

her dress soaked through.)

She wasn't wearing her shoes,

which she'd left in a repair shop across the street.

What a terrible symbol is the payphone.

★

You can tell a man's fortune from the bumps on his head.

★

I want to be buried in a Cadillac.

Maybe you could have loved me.

Valediction

I guess you could say we grew up together.
The party in high school where we met.
First time we ever got drunk.
A girl punched me in the stomach that night
and threw the little ring
I gave her into the bushes.
I never did find it.
And I never found out
who told her I'd been messing around
with the coach's daughter.

All those prank phone calls to Joe Staub.
Who could have answered so many questions
about his sister's anatomy?
A week later he died in a car accident
and we were left with his shrinking voice on tape.
Cruelty was our forte.
Aborted attempts at B & E (we weren't good with locks),
wine stolen from the pizzeria,
Sherman's march through adjoining neighborhoods.
It's amazing what I had the guts to do
and now I can hardly get up the nerve
to ask a stranger what time it is.

Vandalism and larceny weren't going to make us famous,

so we went to college, started the band

we always talked about, honed our drinking skills.

Once, we made an agreement

to stay drunk forty days and forty nights

and not to wash our hair, like two kids

dressed up as bums on Halloween.

You finished school; I didn't.

The music got us out of Ohio

and into a one-room apartment in Hollywood.

One dark room, everything in it shades of green.

We stuck together as long as we could

but there were no adventures,

unless you count passing out

with turkey pot pies in the oven

and setting the kitchen on fire.

After three years I'm something close to sane again.

I'm more on the wagon than off,

and there's an electricity in me.

I've come to a moment

that feels curiously like the moment

just before Thanksgiving dinner

when you're supposed to pray
but this ritual is gone from your life,
and it's dead silent
until someone's fork finally hits a plate.
I don't know what I'm trying to say.
Goodbye, I guess.

Whiskey for Charlie

for J.B. Cheng

I've had my share of last drinks.
This is it, I say to myself,
and order one final scotch to savor
like the last at-bat of an illustrious career.
Only the blood in my veins is ovational.

My grandfather Charlie must have known
the same self-dividedness after the benders
that landed him in Harlan County Hospital.
When I was a boy my father dragged me
down there while he was drying out.
He looked gray and oilless,
his sleeping mouth trying to suckle,
a shell of the man who'd survived being shot
three times at a poker game in Pineville.

Charlie had his last drink this past February.
He fell down, drunk,
in the hunting cabin he lived in
and died of thirst.
He lay there for days.
At 73, he still had a full head of white hair.

Charlie, I never really talked to you.
I wanted you to tell me about the mines.
Was it cold where they sent you
to pick up rocks to heat the world?
Did the black breath of necessity lie to your lungs?

At the funeral his drinking friends
sat on one side of the aisle
and his non-drinking friends sat on the other.
The body in the casket had three bullets in it:
two in the leg and one in the hip.
I wish they had cut one of those slugs out,
so I could hold it in my hand,
something that lives forever,
without eyes, and speaks to me in the Kentucky accent I love
though I'm afraid to admit it.

Any night now, Charlie, I'll walk into a bar,
order a whiskey for you and not drink it.
Because I'd rather pull all my teeth
in front of the bathroom mirror
than keep getting the sawdust kicked out of me.

Jimmy Huber's Lament   *for Reggie Smith*

I'd been working with Dad for about a month, and Mom asked
me to go pick him up one night he was working late. We were
doing the Wilson kid, the one killed in that car wreck on 206?
I remember when they brought his body in. There was a piece
of metal about the size of a chicken wing stuck in his chest.
The car had caught on fire, and he was alive trying to get out–
he had on a pair of Herman Survivors, and the lacings and
upper part fused right to the flesh of his legs. We pulled the
chunk of metal out and scraped the boots off his feet. A wreck
like that, you always imagine it happens at night, but this was in
broad daylight, so the kid's sunglasses were practically melted
onto his face. The family was pretty upset. Thought they were
going to have to close the casket. But Dad concocted some
kind of chemical peel to get the plastic off. When I got to the
shop the body was already in the show room. I stopped to look
at him for a minute. What an incredible job. It's been three
years and I bet you could dig him up right now, scrape off the
mold, and he'd be ready for viewing. I heard Dad in the storage
room and went in there to see if he was ready to go, and he was
painting a casket. I asked him what he was doing, but I realized.
He was putting a coat of copper sealer on a Batesville. With
copper sealer on it a Batesville looks just like a Hanson. Four-
thousand dollars as opposed to a thousand. I guess that's how
he put me through undertaking school.

Connection

Jim Simpson challenged Russell Aber
to a fly-eating contest
in the locker room before football practice
and won 26 to 25.
Russell Aber was a risk-taker.
We had him diving in icy lakes,
drinking vinegar and eating all manner
of insects, dirt, shoe polish—
even ate half a shoe once—
and all he demanded was reverence.
Jim Simpson was an upstart.
After seeing what eating things
had done for Russell's reputation
he, too, craved the uncommon validity
reserved for the charmingly disgusting.
The two of them sat like kings
at opposite sides of the room,
swallowing fly after proffered fly
as everyone gagged and grimaced.
Jim Simpson defeated the great Russell Aber.

That was fifteen years ago,
and I just read a letter from my sister

asking if I remember a kid named Jim Simpson.
She said he'd been down in Georgia
working construction with our father
who, one Sunday, came home
to find his trailer broken into.
Gone were his television, his tools, his sunglasses;
and Simpson didn't show up for work on Monday.
I sat against the wall, wondering
if he thought of me
as he carried my father's valuables away.
Wondering what eating flies
does to a boy's heart.

The Quick

It's waking up in the morning and brushing your teeth
so vigorously the toothbrush snaps in half.
It's thinking you're really on top of things
when in fact the bottom fell out.
It's saying hello to the same people day after day
without ever knowing their names.
It's wishing that windows were made of sugar,
like in the movies.
It's a wristwatch with a crucifixion on its face.
The upright beam is the hour hand;
the transverse beam is the minute hand.
Christ gets all tangled up.
It's apologizing for hitting a bad note in a bad song.
It's slogging around the library until your legs ache.
It's headphones–morning, noon, and night.
It's a praying mantis on a loaf of bread.
It's being addicted to the world.
It's a woman in a two-piece bathing suit on a beach
in Thessaloniki. She sends you stuffed animals in the mail
and you have no idea what to *do* with them.
It's falling in love with the rowing machine.

It's sitting on the end of your bed in a televisionless void,

transfixed.

It's being so sad that breasts don't make sense anymore.

It's elevator buttons and boiled potatoes and elbows.

It's waiting all night for the telephone to ring

and then not answering it when it does.

It's feeling like a human cannonball without a cannon.

It's not the town; it's not the people;

it's horrible is what it is.

It's sticking it out until you're good and stuck.

It's trying to speak without moving your lips.

It's attempting to remove the object of temptation.

It's a damn shame.

It's wasting time grooving to the devouring whims of belly

dancers.

It's frost on the ribs of a radiator.

It's the accumulation of unsatisfactory moments.

It's knowing how easy it would be to take your head

in your hands and break your neck.

P.O. Box in Jersey

My p.o. box is
on the bottom row.
To check it
I crouch down
in the catcher's position,
tilt my head
to the side and peer in.
Same as looking
under a car.
I check it twice a week
which is probably too often
but I don't care.
My p.o. box is
the most stable address
I will ever have.
I'm paying $22 a year.
That works out to $1.83
a month: pretty cheap rent.
If only I were smaller
I could live in it.
It's unfurnished,
but doll house furniture
would do nicely–

a tiny couch and bed,
a little kitchen table.
That huge hand coming in
the back door every day
would be inconvenient,
but life wouldn't be
such a grumble in my p.o. box.
Safe from all my enemies
like a gangster
in a haberdashery.
Did I mention that
it's a perfect rectangle?

The Visit   *for Kerry*

When green cicadas arc and wail
in the morning sun
like armless monks resigned to guard
the handprints on a banister

and church bells pour their various syrups
into the ears of the disconnected,

you will be standing in the road,
weak from tearful rapture,
trying to say goodbye,
trying to come back in and say goodbye,

but a thousand vipers will evangelize
through transparent wings,
so pulsant and alive, not even their blunt corpses
at dusk regret the morning sun.

New Suit, Just Like Mayakovsky

It was two in the afternoon
and I was playing chess
with my sister's live-in boyfriend.
We were both out of work.
He'd been laid off by General Motors
and had three weeks' unemployment left.
I had forty dollars to get me
through the rest of the summer.

"Is it my move?" I said.
"Yeah," he said, draining his beer.
He was a male stripper
before moving in with my sister.
I felt ill at ease around him.
He was always getting rough with me:
wrestling holds and quasi-martial arts stuff.
I'm not sure what he did at GM;
probably he worked on the line.

"We gotta finish this game," he said,
"before your sister gets home."
He was winning again.
I had a rook and a few pawns left.

He had his queen, a knight,
both rooks, a bishop— it was a slaughter.
I borrowed a beer from the fridge
and braced myself for the end.
He wouldn't checkmate my king
until he captured every piece I had.
It was the only decent thing in his life.

A week later my sister broke it off with him,
and he moved back in with his folks.
She didn't like the way
he treated her daughter
and didn't much like him anymore either.
After a few days he returned
wearing a brand new suit
and asked if they could start over;
she stood her ground and told him no.
"Then I'm going to kill myself," he said
and instructed her as to where
and didn't stop her from picking up
the telephone as he marched out.

The police found his body in the park
across from the station.
He'd been a gymnast in high school,
so he stood between the parallel bars
and shot himself not once but *twice*
in the temple with a .32-caliber pistol.
That's determination.
To be wearing a new suit
in your final moments,
just like Mayakovsky,
without ever having heard of Mayakovsky,
even though you're a laid-off auto worker,
woman gone, no victories left in you at 26,
only half in this world now,
birds scattering,
the blue sky in knots above you.